WHAT
DREAM A

BY CLIVE WHICHELOW
AND PAUL HARDMAN

Published in October 1992 by

ABSON
BOOKS

Abson Books Abson Wick Bristol England

ISBN 0 902920 77 4

Printed by Booksprint, Bristol, England

this Bewk is Dedicated
t'all those as luvs Cats
but maybe recanises
a darker side!

'cause bileev it
or not...us cats
dream about—→

WHUMP!

ASCENT OF SHED ROOF
1926 EXPEDITION

"CLICK